KINGFISHER
LONDON & NEW YORK

Copyright © Kingfisher 2010
Published in the United States by Kingfisher,
175 Fifth Ave., New York, NY 10010
Kingfisher is an imprint of Macmillan Children's Books, London.
All rights reserved.

Illustrated by Ray Bryant
Concept by Jo Connor

Distributed in the U.S. by Macmillan, 175 Fifth Ave.,
New York, NY 10010
Distributed in Canada by H.B. Fenn and Company Ltd.,
34 Nixon Road, Bolton, Ontario L7E 1W2

Library of Congress Cataloging-in-Publication data has
been applied for.

ISBN: 978-0-7534-6417-5

Kingfisher books are available for special
promotions and premiums. For details contact:
Special Markets Department, Macmillan,
175 Fifth Avenue, New York, NY 10010.

For more information, please visit
www.kingfisherbooks.com

Printed in China
10 9 8 7 6 5 4 3 2 1
1TR/0510/LFG/UNTD/140MA

WHAT'S IN THIS BOOK?

WHAT. . .

HAVE YOU EVER ASKED YOURSELF WHAT?

It's only natural to be confused by the world around us . . . It is a very complicated and surprising place sometimes! And you'll never understand what's going on around you unless you ask yourself "WHAT?" every now and then.

This is "what" we have included in this book.

We have traveled over the land, under the sea, up mountains, across deserts—and even into outer space—to collect as many tricky questions as we could find . . .

. . . and we also found the answers for you!

We now invite you to come with us on our journey around the world of "WHAT" so that we can show you all the answers we have discovered.

Did you know . . .

Waterspouts can suck up animals and carry them for miles. Fish, frogs, birds, jellyfish, worms, and lizards have all been known to fall from the sky.

While we were searching for all those answers, we found out some other pretty interesting things, too. We wrote them all down on these panels so that you can memorize these facts and impress your friends!

We also thought it might be fun to see how much of this shiny new knowledge you can remember—so at the back of the book, on pages 56 and 57, you'll find some Quick-Quiz questions to test you. It's not as scary as it sounds—we promise it'll be fun. (And besides, we've given you all the answers on pages 58 and 59.)

Are you ready for this big adventure? Then let's go!

WHAT MADE EARLY EXPLORERS STARSTRUCK?

The first explorers didn't have compasses to help them find their way. Instead, they learned how to use the positions of the stars to guide them. They also used the Sun's position to help them during the day.

WHAT WERE THE FIRST CARS LIKE?

Did you know . . .

In the 1800s, when drivers in Great Britain wanted to go out in their cars, someone had to walk in front with a flag to warn other road users!

The first cars were steam engines on wheels— noisy, smoky machines. But these steam cars soon became quicker and easier to drive. They were used for almost 30 years, until they were replaced by faster cars with gasoline engines.

WHAT IS SLEEPWALKING?

Did you know . . .

Some animals, such as ducks, keep one half of their brain awake while the other half sleeps. This is so they are still aware if a predator is nearby.

Some people get out of bed and walk around while they are still asleep. They do not know they are doing it, and when they wake up, they do not remember it, either!

WHAT WAS THE SILK ROAD?

Did you know . . .

For centuries, nobody outside of China knew how silk was made. The punishment for giving away the secret was death.

In 127 B.C., a traveler named Zhang Qian reached central Asia. Centuries afterward, traders began using his route to transport luxury goods between China and Europe. It was named the Silk Road because silk was the most popular luxury item.

WHAT IS THE UNIVERSE?

The universe is an unimaginable area filled with planets, stars, dust, gas, and galaxies. The universe is getting bigger. Galaxies (huge groups of stars) are speeding away from one another—making the universe even larger.

WHAT IS THE MILKY WAY?

The Milky Way is the galaxy in which we live. It has more than one trillion stars, including the Sun, and is shaped like an enormous whirlpool. It rotates once every 200 million years. It is so big that light takes 100,000 years to cross from one side to the other.

Did you know . . .

In the Milky Way, there are almost 200 stars for every person on Earth.

WHAT DO SCIENTISTS DO?

Scientists ask many questions about how and why things happen. They carry out experiments to try to answer these questions and prove their ideas.

12

WHAT IS EVOLUTION?

Evolution is what scientists call the very slow process when one type of living thing changes into another type. The first bacteria were tiny, made up of only one cell, and took more than 2.5 billion years to evolve into larger creatures.

WHAT IS IT LIKE ON THE MOON?

Earth's Moon is dry, dusty, and lifeless.

There is no air to breathe, and it is so hot during the day that your blood would boil. At night, however, it is freezing cold.

WHAT IS IT LIKE IN THE OCEAN?

Did you know . . .
Earthquakes can happen under the sea. There are more than one million earthquakes each year, but most are so deep down that we cannot feel them.

There are mountains and valleys at the bottom of the ocean, just as there are on land. Along the shore, the land slopes gently into the ocean. This slope is called the continental shelf.

15

WHAT IS EARTH MADE OF?

Earth is made up of many layers. Near the center of Earth is the core. It is mainly made up of nickel and iron. Above the core is the mantle, which is a thick layer of rock that is so hot that some of it has melted away. The final layer is the crust, which is what you walk on.

WHAT IS A COUNTRY?

A country is an independent land with its own government. The government runs the country and makes laws, which people must follow. A country has its own name, and its borders are usually agreed to by other countries around the world.

17

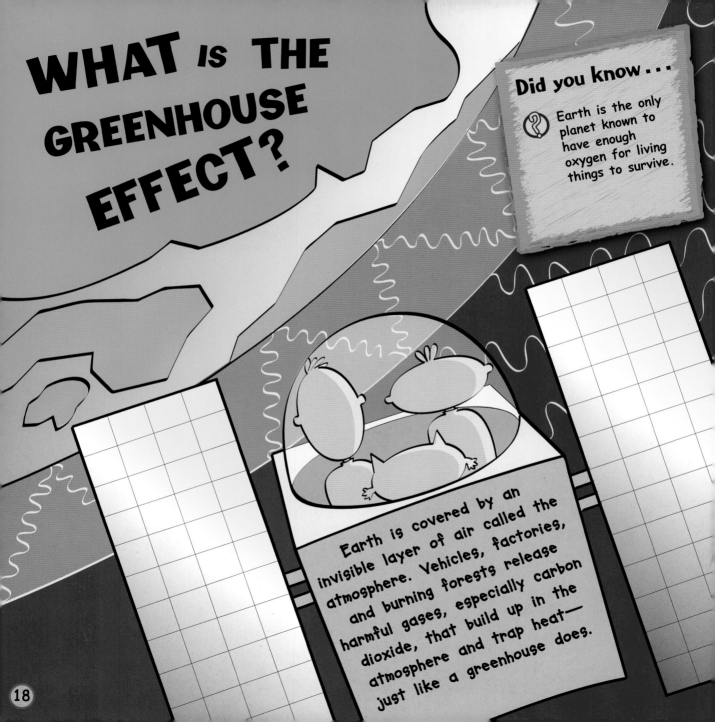

WHAT IS THE GREENHOUSE EFFECT?

Earth is covered by an invisible layer of air called the atmosphere. Vehicles, factories, and burning forests release harmful gases, especially carbon dioxide, that build up in the atmosphere and trap heat—just like a greenhouse does.

WHAT ARE CLOUDS MADE OF?

Did you know...

The biggest clouds are cumulonimbus, reaching 6 miles (9.7 kilometers) high and holding up to half a million tons of water.

Clouds are made up of billions of water droplets and ice crystals that are light enough to float. Clouds form when warm air rises and the water vapor in the air changes from gas to liquid. When billions of these droplets come together, they form a cloud.

WHAT IS AIR MADE OF?

Air is a mixture of gases. It consists mostly of nitrogen and oxygen, but carbon dioxide and water vapor are also present. As well as gases, it also has tiny pieces of salt, dust, and dirt.

Did you know . . .

you don't notice it, but the air around you is heavy. You never feel its weight on you because it is constantly moving.

WHAT IS THUNDER?

Thunder is a sound caused by lightning. Sparks of lightning are very hot. As they flash through the sky, they heat the air so quickly that it expands very rapidly. The expansion of air is what causes the noise of thunder.

Did you know . . .

The biggest thunderclouds tower 10 miles (16 kilometers) into the air. That's almost twice the height of Mount Everest in Asia!

WHAT IS LIGHTNING?

In a thundercloud, small pieces of ice bump into one another as they move around in the air. All of these collisions create a huge charge of electricity. This charge is released in brilliant flashes of lightning.

Did you know...

Lightning is so hot that it can melt sand. As the sand cools, it forms a glassy sculpture of the lightning's flash path.

WHAT IS IT LIKE AT THE POLES?

The North Pole (the Arctic) and the South Pole (Antarctica) are at the very ends of Earth. They are freezing cold places that are covered in ice and snow. Only the toughest animals live there.

24

WHAT WERE THE ICE AGES?

Did you know...

The last ice age was almost 12,000 years ago and was called the Great Ice Age. Almost one-third of Earth was covered in ice!

The ice ages were periods of time when it was so cold that snow and ice covered huge areas of Earth. They began two million years ago, and there have been 11 ice ages in total. People used to live in caves and wear animal fur to stay warm.

WHAT WIND CAN SINK A SHIP?

Did you know . . .

Hurricane winds roar at more than 73 miles (117 kilometers) per hour. They start above warm tropical seas and bring very heavy rain and howling winds.

Hurricanes are not only dangerous on land—they can also cause destruction out at sea. Hurricane winds can whip up a 98-foot- (30-meter-) high wall of water. When a wave of this size and power smashes down, it can sink a ship in minutes.

WHAT MAKES WAVES ROLL?

Waves are ripples of water blown across the surface of the ocean by the wind. On a calm day, they hardly move. In stormy weather, they roll faster and higher until they form huge walls of water.

Did you know...

In Waimea Bay, Hawaii, surfers ride waves up to 33 feet (10 meters) high!

WHAT IS A CORAL REEF?

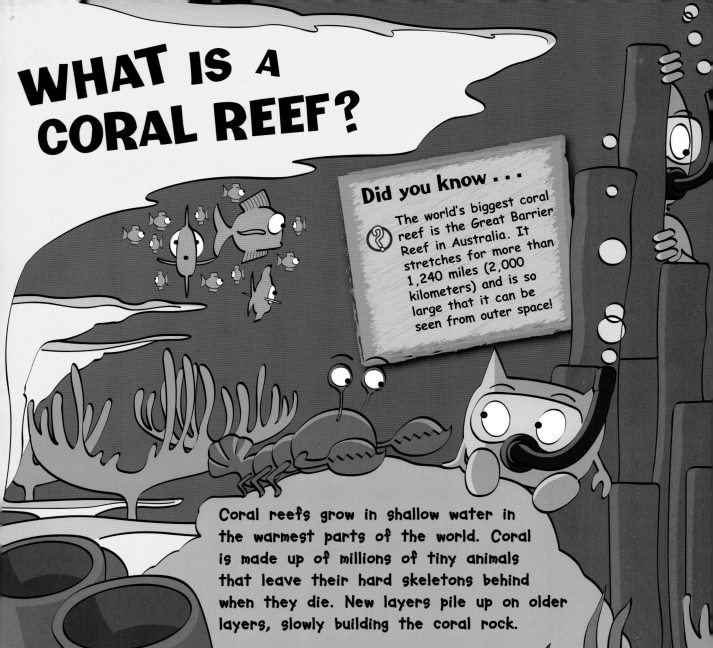

Did you know . . .

The world's biggest coral reef is the Great Barrier Reef in Australia. It stretches for more than 1,240 miles (2,000 kilometers) and is so large that it can be seen from outer space!

Coral reefs grow in shallow water in the warmest parts of the world. Coral is made up of millions of tiny animals that leave their hard skeletons behind when they die. New layers pile up on older layers, slowly building the coral rock.

Sharks and dolphins belong to two very different animal groups. Dolphins are mammals, which means they breathe air through their lungs and their babies drink their mothers' milk. Sharks are fish, so they breathe through gills and use their fins to move.

WHAT IS INSIDE MY HEAD?

Underneath your hair, skin, and hard skull bone is your brain. This organ controls almost everything you do. It tells you to blink, remembers directions, and makes you think.

Did you know . . .

Your brain has two sides. The right side helps you think about things such as music, colors, and shapes. The left side of your brain helps you with math, puzzles, and speech.

WHAT IS A DREAM?

Did you know . . .

Many animals dream when they are asleep. Dogs sometimes twitch their legs as if they are dreaming of chasing something!

A dream is a story that your brain makes up while you are asleep. It feels as if it is actually happening. Dreams can involve many different emotions—happiness, sadness, or fear. Scary dreams are called nightmares.

WHAT DOES MY HEART DO?

Did you know...

The heart has two sides. The right side pumps blood to the lungs. The left side pumps blood around the body.

Your heart is a muscle that keeps your blood moving. If you put your hand on your chest, close to your heart, you can feel it beating. Each time it beats, it pumps blood all around your body.

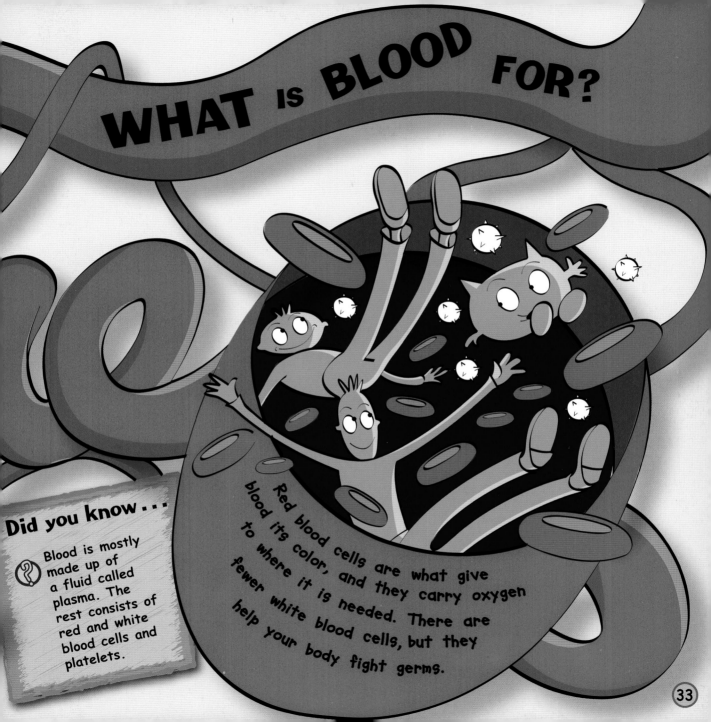

WHAT is BLOOD FOR?

Red blood cells are what give blood its color, and they carry oxygen to where it is needed. There are fewer white blood cells, but they help your body fight germs.

Did you know...

Blood is mostly made up of a fluid called plasma. The rest consists of red and white blood cells and platelets.

WHAT ARE GERMS?

Germs are tiny living things that are too small to see. There are billions of them on and in you all the time. Most germs will not hurt you, but some can make you sick. When this happens, your blood gets to work and kills them, making you feel better again.

WHAT WAS THE BLACK DEATH?

The Black Death was a terrible sickness that we call a plague. It began in the 1330s and spread from Asia to Europe, carried by rats. The rats had tiny fleas that passed on the plague when they bit people. In only 13 years, the Black Death had killed up to 200 million people.

WHAT LEAPS UP WATERFALLS?

Did you know . . .

Some salmon have been known to swim and leap 2,000 miles (3,200 kilometers) to get back to the river where they were born.

Atlantic salmon spend most of their life at sea, but they swim back to the river where they were born when it is time to breed (have offspring). They swim against the flow of the river and can even leap up waterfalls.

WHAT IS A **LEAP YEAR?**

Every four years, a leap year occurs. This is when a year has 366 days instead of 365. This extra day is added to the end of February. So if your birthday is February 29, you were born in a leap year.

WHAT IS A BLOWHOLE?

When seawater rises at high tide, waves rush into caves and pound against their roofs. The power of the waves is so strong that they can make a hole in the roof of a cave. This is a blowhole. When waves crash into the cave again, they shoot out of the blowhole.

WHAT IS A WATERSPOUT?

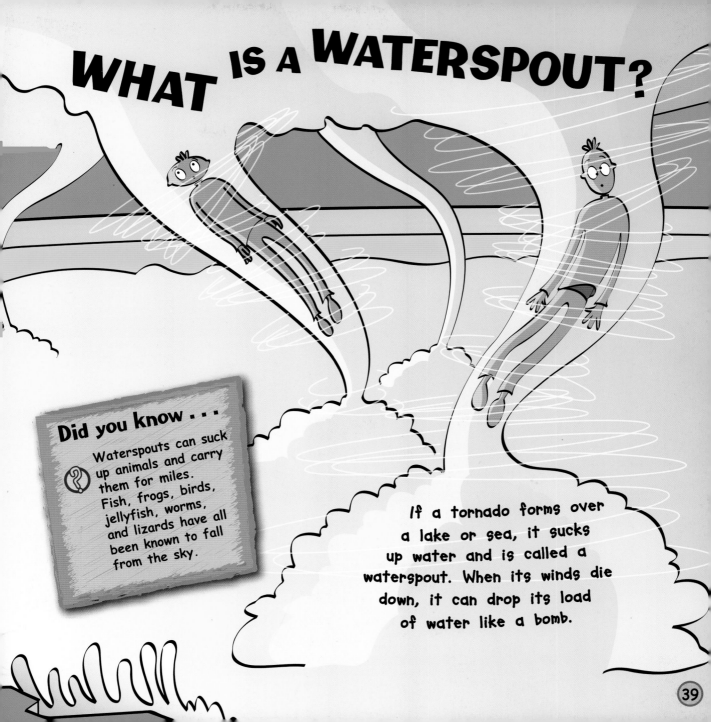

Did you know . . .

Waterspouts can suck up animals and carry them for miles. Fish, frogs, birds, jellyfish, worms, and lizards have all been known to fall from the sky.

If a tornado forms over a lake or sea, it sucks up water and is called a waterspout. When its winds die down, it can drop its load of water like a bomb.

WHAT MAKES LAND SLIDE?

Did you know . . .

An avalanche occurs when snow breaks away from a mountain and crashes downhill. This can be caused by an earthquake— or even by a very loud noise.

Landslides take place when soil and rocks slide down a slope together at fast speed. They can be caused by heavy rainfall, which can make the slope weaker. Sometimes these landslides are small, but other times they can be enormous and involve the whole side of a mountain.

WHAT GIVES EARTH THE SHAKES?

Did you know . . .

Earthquakes can occur under the sea. When this happens, a huge wave calld a tsunami travels across the sea.

Earth is made up of huge pieces of flat rock called tectonic plates. These plates move very slowly. The place where they meet is called a fault. When the plates rub together, shock waves travel through the ground, causing tremors and shakes.

41

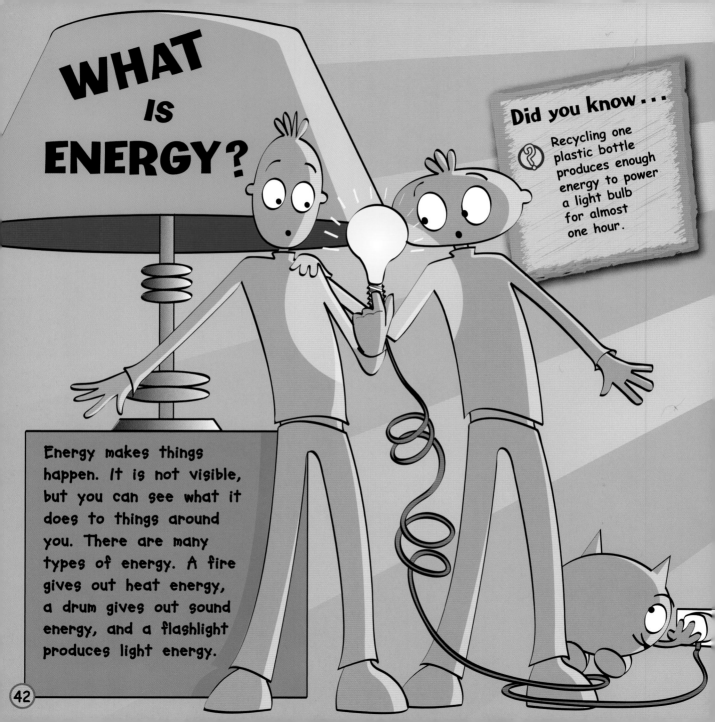

WHAT IS ENERGY?

Energy makes things happen. It is not visible, but you can see what it does to things around you. There are many types of energy. A fire gives out heat energy, a drum gives out sound energy, and a flashlight produces light energy.

WHAT ARE STALACTITES AND STALAGMITES?

Did you know . . .

Stalactites are never as large as stalagmites. That's because as a stalactite gets bigger, it becomes too heavy and crashes to the ground.

Stalactites and stalagmites are spectacular, strong structures that sometimes form inside limestone caves. Both are carrot shaped, but while stalactites hold tight to a cave roof, stalagmites are mounted on the cave floor.

WHAT IS A TROLL?

In Viking and Scandinavian legends, trolls are big, strong, and scary creatures that live in caves. They appear only at night to hunt for their favorite dinner—humans!

WHAT ARE STARS MADE OF?

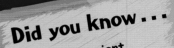

Did you know...

Since ancient times, people have seen patterns in the way that stars are grouped. These patters are called constellations.

Stars are huge balls of gas that include gases that are also in the air around you. The two main gases in stars are hydrogen and helium. They are called the stars' fuel, and stars make heat and light from them.

WHAT IS A BLACK HOLE?

A black hole can happen when a massive star dies. The star falls in on itself, squashing together all of its material, and becomes smaller and smaller. In the end, all that's left is a place that even light cannot escape from—a black hole.

Did you know...

Everything in space has a pulling force called gravity. This force holds things together and stops them from floating away into space.

47

WHAT DID EGYPTIAN WRITING LOOK LIKE?

48

Did you know...

Some Egyptian boys trained as scribes—their job was writing. They had to learn more than 700 hieroglyphs.

The first Egyptian writing was made up of rows of pictures called hieroglyphs. Each picture represented a sound, object, action, idea, feeling, or number.

WHAT IS PREHISTORY?

Did you know...

The first writing system was invented by people called the Sumerians, who lived in the area now known as the Middle East.

Prehistory is the time before there were any written records about things that happened in the world. We know about prehistoric life through fossils—the remains of animals and plants that died millions of years ago.

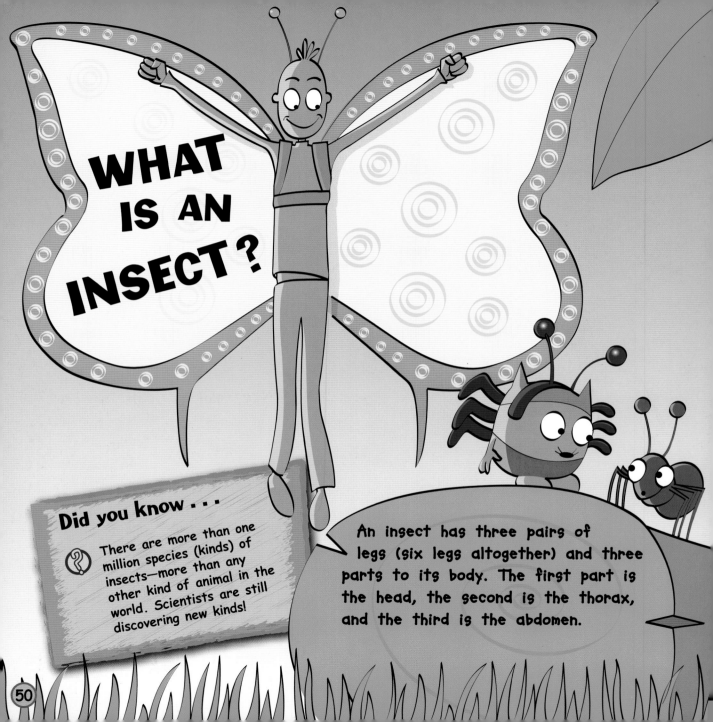

WHAT IS A BUG?

Did you know...

People who study insects are called entomologists. They travel around the world, learning about insects and trying to protect them.

Bugs are insects that have needlelike beaks, such as stinkbugs and aphids. A bug uses its beak to cut open its food. Then it sucks up the tasty juices inside, using its beak like a straw.

WHAT IS THE DIFFERENCE BETWEEN FROGS AND TOADS?

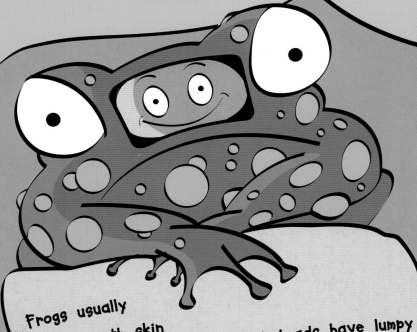

Did you know...

Frogs and toads are both amphibians. This means they are cold-blooded, have a backbone, and live in damp places both in and out of the water.

Frogs usually have smooth skin and long legs for leaping. Most toads have lumpy skin and move their short, thick bodies by crawling.

WHAT WALKS ON WATER?

Did you know...

The common basilisk (also known as the Jesus Christ lizard) runs so fast that it can cross rivers and lakes without sinking.

Water striders are tiny insects that are so light that they can walk on water. But they wouldn't get anywhere without a force called surface tension. This pulls at the surface of the water, making a thin, stretchy "skin" on the top.

WHAT DID PEOPLE USE BEFORE FRIDGES?

Did you know . . .

People used to make natural refrigerators by lining caves and holes with a thick layer of snow in the winter. These icehouses kept fresh food cool throughout the summer.

Electric refrigerators were invented around 1920. Before then, people kept their food in a wooden cupboard called an icebox. Huge blocks of ice would keep the cupboard cool.

QUICK-QUIZ QUESTIONS

1. How long ago was the compass invented?

2. What name was given to the route used by traders to transport goods between China and Europe?

3. What galaxy do we live in?

4. Unscramble SOUR TULIP SEA to spell the name of a famous scientist.

5. How long does it take the Moon to orbit Earth?

6. What is the world's smallest country?

7. What is the largest organ of your body?

8. What are the main gases in air?

9. Lightning is very cold. True or false?

10. Where do polar bears live?

11. How fast can hurricane winds travel?

12. Where is the Great Barrier Reef?

13. Which side of your brain helps with math and puzzles?

14. What is plasma?

15. When did the Black Death begin?

16. How often does a leap year occur?

17. Unscramble WAS TO ERUPT to spell what a tornado turns into when it is over water.

18. What are the huge pieces of flat rock in Earth called?

19. Name an example of renewable energy.

20. Stalactites hang down from cave roofs. True or false?

21. What are the patterns of stars called?

22. Unscramble ROLE SPY HIGH to spell the first type of Egyptian writing.

23. How many pairs of legs do insects have?

24. What force pulls at the surface of water?

25. Why is buying food grown locally good for the environment?

QUICK-QUIZ ANSWERS

1. More than 1,000 years ago.

2. The Silk Road.

3. The Milky Way.

4. SOUR TULIP SEA = Louis Pasteur.

5. About 27 days.

6. Vatican City.

7. Your skin.

8. The main two gases are nitrogen and oxygen.

9. False. It is very hot.

10. In the Arctic.

11. At more than 73 miles (117 kilometers) per hour.

12. In Australia.

13. The left side.

14. The fluid in blood.

15. In the 1300s.

16. Every four years.

17. WAS TO ERUPT = waterspout.

18. Tectonic plates.

19. Energy from water, wind, or the Sun is renewable.

20. True. Stalagmites form on a cave floor.

21. Constellations.

22. ROLE SPY HIGH = hieroglyphs.

23. Three pairs (six legs).

24. Surface tension.

25. Because fewer food miles are produced.

TRICKY WORDS

AMPHIBIANS
Animals, such as frogs, that can live both on land and in water.

ATMOSPHERE
The layer of gases surrounding a planet. Earth's atmosphere holds in the heat from the Sun but also keeps out many of its harmful rays.

AZTECS
The people who lived in central Mexico from 700 to 500 years ago.

BACTERIA
Types of germs that can cause illness (singular: bacterium).

CARBON DIOXIDE
A colorless, invisible gas that animals breathe out. Carbon dioxide is also made by burning fossil fuels, such as coal and oil.

CELL
The smallest part of an animal or plant. All living things are made up of cells.

ENVIRONMENT
The natural world—the sea, land, and all the living things—on the planet.

EXPAND
To become larger.

FINS
Winglike parts on a fish's body. Fins move to push the fish through the water and keep it balanced.

FLEA
A small, jumping insect that feeds on blood.

GALAXY
A huge system of millions or billions of stars. The stars, along with gas and dust, are held together by the force of gravity.

GAS
Something that isn't solid or liquid. Oxygen is a gas.

GERM
A tiny living thing that can cause disease.

GILLS
The breathing parts on a fish. Water is taken in through gills, which absorb oxygen in the water and get rid of carbon dioxide.

GOVERNMENT
The group of people who make decisions on how a country is run.

GRAVITY
A force of attraction between objects. This happens in space—for example, when a moon is held in orbit around a planet because the planet is more massive.

LEGEND
A story that has been told to people for a long time and has become part of history but that may not be true.

LUNGS
Organs in the body that help creatures breathe by supplying them with oxygen.

MOON
A large, ball-shaped object that orbits a planet.

NICKEL
A silver-colored metal.

ORBIT
The path of an object as it travels around a larger object. Earth orbits the Sun.

ORGAN
A part of the body that has an important job to do. The skin is an organ that protects the inside of your body, and the heart is an organ that pumps blood around the body.

OXYGEN
A colorless, invisible gas in air that animals need to breathe in order to live.

PLANET
A large, ball-shaped object in space that orbits a star. Earth is a planet.

PREDATOR
An animal that hunts and eats other animals.

REEF
A long line of rock, sand, or coral that lies just beneath the surface of the ocean.

SILK
Fine threads that are made by insects and woven together to make a soft, smooth, and strong material.

SKELETON
The framework of bones in a body.

SMALLPOX
A serious disease that killed many people but that has been wiped out because of a successful vaccine.

TORNADO
A fast and dangerous whirling column of wind shaped like a funnel.

TREMOR
A small earthquake.

TROPICAL
Describes the very hot and damp area around the center of Earth.

VACCINE
A substance given to people, usually by injection, to stop them from developing a particular disease.

VAPOR
A mass of tiny droplets of water in the air that appears as mist or steam.

VISIBLE
Describes something that can be seen.

61